HOW TO INVEST IN UK PROPERTY

At The Best Prices
And Best Financing Rates
Available

Even if you are not British

By *Jorge Lombana & Noel Cardona*

HOW TO INVEST IN UK PROPERTY

As Seen On TV

At The Best Prices And Best Financing Rates Available

Even if you are not British

by Jorge Lombana & Noel Cardona

By Jorge Lombana & Noel Cardona Copyright © 2020

All rights reserved. This book or any portion thereof may not be reproduced or used in any manner whatsoever without the express written permission of the publisher except for the use of brief quotations in a book review or scholarly journal.

First Printing: 2020

978-1-716-28035-1

How to Invest In UK Property at the Best Prices and Best Financing Rates Available

Publisher: Property Strategist Ltd
www.propertystrategist.co.uk

Disclaimer

The information in this book is for educational purposes only. The contents do not constitute financial advice in anyway. You should seek Independent professional advice before making any investment. Investing in property can be risky business just like any other investment. Historical growth in property prices does not mean necessarily that prices will increase in the future. Your property may be repossessed if you do not keep up payments on your mortgage.

I would like thank my clients who have been kind enough to entrust their financial future to us. I hope that their journeys in property is a very successful one. I continue to value their trust in me and the knowledge they have gained through my advice.

I would like to thank Noel Cardona of valuable content, without whom this book would still be just and idea.

Noel demonstrated a lot of patience and professionalism in dealing with all the behind the scenes of the book.

I would like to thank my partner Zuly Baez for her constant support and love through my journey and to understand how important and difficult this has been.

And finally I would like to thank my business partner Chen Lev for the incredible support while we set up the operation and the platform in Liverpool and for his continued assistance and loyalty to me.

Jorge Lombana

To all those entrepreneurs and investors who are looking for freedom and wealth. The latter not only meaning money but a life lived with purpose and intention. Because that is the only way to take control over your destiny.

To my Gio for her love and amazing support.

Noel Cardona

ONE OF MANY SATISFIED INVESTORS...

Having worked as an accountant for over 15 years I always wanted to invest some money in Property.

I knew Jorge was very involved in property and decided to have a chat with him about how I could start investing in property.

Jorge was very helpful and straight forward, he explained the different types of properties that can be purchased and the different strategies used.

He then recommended that I start low and build up as I gain some experience. He helped me along the way to research the market and spot the right type of house to buy.

He then showed me what to look for and shared some of his experiences with me so I didn't make any costly mistakes along the way.

I then ended up buying my first property and rented it within 3 days!!! The whole experience has been amazing and there are highs and lows but honestly it's been a fantastic experience and I am looking forward to buying more houses in the future.

Andres Sanchez
London

THE VALUE STORED HERE

A case study as seen on the BBC--*1*
Learn the Property Language------------------------------------- *3*
The dirty little secret of investing in Property------------------------ *7*
The Right Mindset--*11*
One of the scariest things in Property-------------------------------*13*
Why invest in UK Property Anyway-------------------------------*15*
Current Prices for Property in UK--------------------------------*17*
What Budget to start --*21*
3 secrets to invest in UK Property--------------------------------*23*
Investing in the UK for Non-British Nonresidents------------------*29*
4 strategies to boost your profits---------------------------------*35*
How I achieved Financial Freedom in 4 years----------------------*41*
Creative ways of raising capital---------------------------------*45*
Spotting the Right Location in UK-------------------------------*47*
What can go wrong? --*51*
More about Your Power Team ------------------------------------*55*
Type of Financing Available-------------------------------------*59*
You want to invest but don't have the experience--------------------*63*
Four Successful Investment examples----------------------------*67*
Have We Answered The Question? --------------------------------*71*
What investors are saying --------------------------------------- *73*
Jorge Lombana – Who am I anyway? -----------------------------*75*
Noel Cardona – Who am I anyway? -----------------------------------*83*

A CASE STUDY AS SEEN ON THE BBC
HOMES UNDER THE HAMMER

By Jorge Lombana

Our company has performed well enough to have been featured on **BBC One Homes under the Hammer,** so I thought: why not starting this book with a case study where other experts in UK Property Investments show what we are doing?

I believe it's important you go and see the study case which will give you a unique insight as to how the whole process works.

Go to:

www.propertystrategist.co.uk/realestatetv

BEFORE WE EVEN START...
LEARN THE 'PROPERTY LANGUAGE'

By Noel Cardona

If you are a seasoned investor in Property, skip this chapter.

Every time I get into a new business venture, I look for the common words that niche uses and you should do the same because in business communication is everything and the language of each business is, on many occasions, used to cut outsiders out of the conversation.

Property Equity: The percentage of the property you own. For example, if you have paid 25% for a property that is your equity.

Loan to Value: The money a lender will offer you according to the valuation of a property. If your property is valued at £100,000, the loan you can get will be based on a percentage of that value, i.e. 75%.

Bridge Loan: A loan to be paid in a short time (from 6 months to 2 years) and with higher interest than normal. It is called a bridge loan because helps you 'cross to the other side' and start or continue with your projects. They have the advantage of being approved faster than normal mortgages.

Refurbishing: In the sense of this book, refurbishing means the careful planning and execution of the upgrade of a property aiming to increase both its valuation and cash flow potential. This is normally achieved by optimizing space to increase the number of rooms in the property.

Remortgage: If you bought a property and got a mortgage for £100,000, then fixed it, increasing the valuation to £200,000, you might ask the bank for a second mortgage (remortgage) the property on the new value. The bank will then lend you 75% of £200,000 that is £150,000. As you already had a £100,000 mortgage you have created £50,000 out of the blue.

Cash Flow: Recurrent income from rent.

Return on Investment (ROI):

Annual Rent / (Purchase + Refurbishing Costs)*100

Potential Capital Gains: The increase in the valuation of the property once it has been refurbished.

HMO: House in Multiple Occupation. As defined by the UK government, this is a property where three or more people, not belonging to one family, live together sharing common facilities such as kitchen, toilet and bath rooms.

Council: The UK government has a complex structure of local governments created to be able to delegate responsibility and increase operational efficiency. Whereas this ensures services are well maintained, you will have to deal with different specific rules depending on the area in which you buy your property, especially if you are dealing with HMOs.

Council Tax: a monthly tax setup in the UK to cover the costs of the local government or councils.

Stamp Duty: A tax applied during the purchase of a property. The higher the price of the property the higher the stamp duty to be paid.

THE DIRTY LITTLE SECRET OF INVESTING IN PROPERTY

(And not other type of businesses)

By Noel Cardona

Each type of asset is different. Each of them has its own weaknesses and strengths. For example, there are many businesses which require almost no money to be started (low entry barrier ones) allowing you to invest your time and effort and making it grow. The disadvantage is the normal competition in those kinds of businesses is quite high. Property is the opposite as it is a capital intensive one.

Now, you cannot get into Property as easily. You either need to have the capital or be able to raise it. That can be done either from other investors or even from the seller of the property.

Another unique characteristic of property is the massive financial leverage that it allows you to create.

Professional investors work with what I call the Lombana Property Speed Cycle (LPSC).

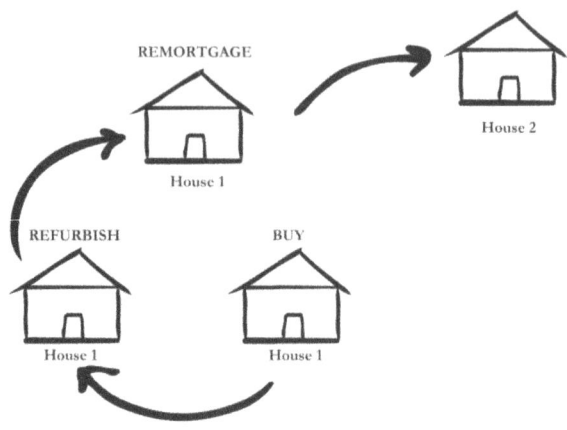

Figure 1. Lombana Property Speed Cycle

In the LPSC, you buy a property at the lowest possible price (auction comes to mind), invest some money to refurbish it. Done correctly, the upgrade should increase the value of the property.

An example we show at the end of the book is this one:

37 Valley Road
Purchase price £70k
3 bedrooms and 1 bathroom
Converted into 5 bedrooms and 2 bathrooms HMO
New value price: £135K

An increase of almost 95% in valuation.

The property was mortgaged and another £60K was acquired while keeping the first one rented and producing cash flow.

That is the LPSC cycle right there working at its best.

In property there are other types of leverage you normally use:

a. Down payment: You get leverage by using other people's money. Other people meaning: family or friends, investors and bank money from unsecured credit.

b. Loan to Value money (basically your mortgage) which is money from the bank taking the house itself as a security.

THE RIGHT MINDSET

By Jorge Lombana

As in any endeavor in business, you need to have the mindset of a winner. You can't just start thinking 'I might not do it', 'I may fail', or 'but what if this happens', or 'actually about what if I don't do this or if I don't do that'.

All you need to do is just handle your risk management and understand that everything is a risk, everything takes time and effort to make it happen. Once you're comfortable with that, once you understand the market (and that's what the research is about), understand your mortgage and what you're doing, you can make that educated decision and decide 'Yes, I am going to do it'.

Having that mindset and absolute clarity of what you want to achieve will give you the resilience required to go through the process. Especially if it's your first investment.

Many of our investors have used our strategies to achieve financial freedom. That in turn has given them the time to explore new things in life, such as travel without worrying about the financial side. They have understood that relying on having the same income for the next 20- 30 years is not an option. They were not prepared to risk 20, 30 years of their life under somebody else dictating what they should earn, they decided to take the risk and start their own entrepreneurial journey.

It is important to make sure your mind is focusing on what you're going to do and ensure you have a 'why':

- Why you want to do this?
- Why you want to choose it?

Have your target clear because once you know where to go and how to get there, you can make a plan which is the most important thing. If you don't have a target, you don't have a 'why' you will become an easy prey to fear and your risk tolerance will go down.

It's like being on a ship without a map and clear coordinates of where you are going. You will be drifting without reaching your destination.

ONE OF THE SCARIEST THINGS IN PROPERTY FOR THE BEGINNER INVESTOR

By Noel Cardona

Continuing from the 'Right Mindset' advice from Jorge, I can tell you from experience that one that of the scariest things a beginner investor will face, to really invest as a professional in Property is this:

Dealing with the mental impact of having tremendous amounts of financial leverage.

What I mean by this is: if you have 10 houses each, one with a mortgage of £100,000, you will be £1,000,000 in debt.

The more financial leverage you have the more your mind will start playing tricks on you. That is where fear may kick in.

What I am saying between lines is that fear is not only exclusive to the newbie investor, but that seasoned investors, given a big enough challenge, will also feel it.

That is why you must ensure you create healthy projects from the beginning creating as much cash flow as possible at high speed, buying at the best possible prices and surrounding yourself with the best power team you can afford.

Also, as you increase the amount of assets you control (own); you finances become more and more complex, which you must become a master at handling. When growing your portfolio (especially if you are doing so rapidly) there will be times where you literally have to 'rob Peter to pay Paul' to juggle cash flow challenges. Jorge and I have plenty of those stories to tell.

WHY INVEST IN UK PROPERTY ANYWAY?

By Noel Cardona

Some people would ask about whether or not after Brexit the UK economy (as of the writing of this book the UK government had not managed to make the transition) will be stop being as strong as it is shown to be.

My answer is, it may do, but after a while it will recover and the most important aspect to keep in mind is that chaos is good if you have cash available: professional investors go out shopping during times of uncertainty, wannabes wait until the conditions are 'good'.

In the same way that if you invest in the stock market, there is more money to be made when uncertainty hits causing panic and stocks to go down very rapidly, any uncertainty caused by political situations is good if used accordingly.

Moving on…

The UK's economy is one of the most stable and strongest in the world (it is categorized as one of the big 5). Employment rates are high, corruption is very low and most importantly, it's a country with no bureaucracy. All those are ingredients to create a good place to hold property.

CURRENT PRICES FOR PROPERTY IN THE UK

By Noel Cardona

It is important to know your battlefield. And as they say in property, location makes a big difference.

However, in this case, I will like to show you what is happening in the UK with property prices. There is a massive difference depending on where you go if you see the map in below, you can clearly see that property in London is leading the way with prices at sometimes more than double that of other places in UK.

The first conclusion you can easily get from here is that if you have limited funds to invest and want good prices, then you may be better off looking outside London.

Current Prices For Property In The UK

Figure 2. UK property simplified price map for 3 bedroom houses

Bear in mind the prices shown above are quite general. The most important thing I wanted to show you is the peaks and valleys so you can see from a distance. In the next chapter we will talk more about budgets.

Some of you will say: 'Well, what you need to focus on property in your Return on Investment and no so much the initial price'... And I agree with that, however, if you are just starting out and struggle to get the money for your first down payment, then this is what you would be looking at.

Now, to make things even better, the prices presented above are market prices and nowhere near the ones you could currently get if you use the types of strategies we present in this book.

WHAT BUDGET SHOULD I HAVE TO START INVESTING IN PROPERTY IN THE UK?

By Jorge Lombana

It all depends on the property itself, so as I said, outside London, I mean places like northwest England such as Halcrow, Liverpool, and Manchester, you still can find some places.

For example, for a 2-bedroom property, you're looking at something around £60,000. For a 3-bedroom, you're looking roughly at something around £90,000. Now, that would be a property that requires refurbishment, which potentially could cost you, anything between twenty to thirty grand (20,000 – 30,000) on top of it.

So, once you've got the initial deposit for the property and the budget for the refurbishment, then you could have your potential property ready to rent in the market and the start of getting income out of it.

Although, the type of investors that we currently work with are retired people, somewhere in their 60's or 70's that have already worked their entire life and have some pension funds that they would like to withdraw or some money saved on the side.

Also, employed people who are currently working and have some savings, and just some general business or investors that are interested in getting into the property market. Some of them already have some properties but they don't have the time to look for new properties and doing the whole process again. They just want to delegate that side and that is how we find these investors and potentially take the work load from them. Hence, offering a full package where they can just rely on our service to source the property, go through the legal side to purchase it, do the project management of the refurbishment and rent it out once it's all completed. Thus the investor will receive the passive income from the property.

3 SECRETS TO INVEST IN UK PROPERTY

By Jorge Lombana

The first and most important secret is this one:

Do Your Research

You must know exactly how much house prices are in the area where you're looking to invest.

Look for comparisons, for what I call value points:

- Schools, universities and hospitals nearby.
- Potential developments that are happening in the area.
- Potential investments that will come. All planning applications that have been submitted to the council (UK local government).

So now you know exactly what's going on in that area for the next 5-10 years. With focused effort and dedication you can discover areas that, at the moment, are not the best, but have a huge potential for growth within the next few years.

Also the demand on the rentals is important to know: how much you can rent the property for and if there is enough potential and demand in the area to rent it out quickly. We need to have the properties rented at all times and if you don't pick the right property in the right area, it may take you a long time to do so, which is obviously a big problem.

So, to avoid all this, you need to do your research and make sure that what you're buying has enough potential.

The second secret is this one:

HAVE A POWER TEAM

You need to have a very good support team: have the legal side covered, somebody who can find the properties for you, or, if you've got the time, you could potentially be doing yourself a favor by building good relationships with local Estate Agents and people in the area. Obviously those are the ones that are going to supply you with properties so you can play the game of speed in Property which is this one:

By the time a new property comes up, before even goes to the market you'll already know about it.

This on its own will give you a massive advantage over other investors.

Secret number three is to

HAVE YOUR FINANCING IN PLACE.

There are a lot of people who say that with no money down you can buy properties. However it's very optimistic to think that way. In my experience, you always need to have some money set aside to pay for legals, refurbishment, furniture etc. Let me point this out for you; when finding the right opportunity you need the cash to be invested immediately, therefore you should have the money ready or be able to raise the funds fairly quickly. These 3 rules of thumb are probably some the most insightful ones and that's how I built my portfolio in the last few years.

TOOLS TO DO YOUR RESEARCH

Doing research on a property is basically going on apps or websites such as **Zoopla, Rightmove, On the Market.com,** government websites of local councils to see what plans and any relevant information about the area, check the demographics and population of that particular area you are investing in to understand the potential demand for properties; visit spareroom.com to see how many people are actively looking for rooms or flats in the area.

You will also find out the potential rent you can expect once the property is refurbished. Furthermore, you can **open up maps in Google** and just research the area about shops, restaurants, bars, highest routes, local schools, and transport links, proximity to the city center, companies, and hospitals. The reason behind this analysis is to have a clear understanding of the area and the potential it has before you make your investment.

Property Prices Follow Jobs

For example, hospitals and big companies employ a lot of people and those people need to live **somewhere close** to where they work, so having a hospital near your house is one of the biggest advantages because you know it's going to fill the demand on the rental side.

TARGET TENANTS VS TYPE OF PROPERTY AND LOCATION

One of the rules of thumb in this business, is to know who you're targeting, so if you're going to buy a property close to a university you would know that you're going to have plenty of students throughout the year to fill your property. On that basis you know they don't have enough money to pay for a whole house, so you could potentially divide the property and convert it into a House in Multiple Occupation (HMO) and then rent each individual room to students. From experience you can potentially make a lot more money that way. Another case for example, is if you buy somewhere more residential where you have more families.

Your property has to be designed and refurbished thinking about your target tenant. For example, if you were targeting families you must think about good spaces and have good standards for living, whereas with students, all they need is super-fast broadband, super modern decoration and good standards without going over the top because they are known to not look after the place the live in. You can't really just go all the way if the property is going to be an HMO. In this case I just recommend investing the minimum required to make it attractive to a student but don't go overboard with it.

Wealthy areas will require a different approach to the design and targeting of potential tenants with rentals being a lot higher. To focus on such properties you will need to look for specific neighborhoods. If you're targeting students, the property will need to include more bathrooms and as many rooms as possible so you can maximize your return on investment.

In Summary, you need to know who you're targeting to before you even start investing. Just make sure you have your research done, that you know what other potential tenants that you're going to find, and once you have that, you need to know exactly how much money you're going to charge for rent, so you can forecast what your potential return investment will be before you decide to invest your money.

INVESTING IN THE UK FOR NON BRITISH – NON RESIDENT INDIVIDUALS

By Noel Cardona

When you invest in a place which you normally live far away from, i.e., investing in the UK but living in Israel, apart from the normal questions on taxation when buying and selling and access to local financing, etc, you must also think about the maintenance of the property, rent collection and payment of ongoing taxes such as the council tax. You are effectively creating a living and breathing business which needs attention.

So the question is: Can you, as a non-British non-resident individual, buy property in the UK? The answer is yes, you can! And it can be done either as an individual or as company. This has profound implications in your exit strategy. For example, a nonresident buying as an individual will be subject to Inheritance tax, where as a non-resident's company won't

THE BUYING PROCESS

When buying UK property, all the due diligence on a property must be done before entering into a binding contract. What this means is, for example, activities such as checking who the owner is, obtaining a survey, carrying out searches of local or other authorities, obtaining information from the buyer and agreeing to the terms of the contract. This is a tricky process for which you need a good local solicitor who knows his/her way through the UK's Property arena.

As a non-resident, you'll be expected to have comprehensive paperwork for the application process (such as passport, proof of creditworthiness and mortgage affordability) and can expect to pay various fees to arrange one (typically in excess of £2,000). You will typically need a sizeable deposit to access a UK mortgage (upwards of 25%) and will need to demonstrate that you can obtain enough rental income from the tenant to cover the interest on the mortgage. The amount you can borrow will depend on how much rent the property can generate, but lenders will typically require your expected rental income to meet at least 125% of the monthly interest payments on the loan. If you intend to use this route (getting a UK mortgage) you will need a formal offer.

Once the contracts are signed the solicitor will do the formal 'exchange of contracts'. At this point the buyer pays a deposit between 5 and 10%.

From there it can take up to 28 days to complete all matters. Once ready, your solicitor will indicate that the balance must be paid upon which the title is transferred and allowing you to can take full possession of the property.

This is a complex process. Something we normally do is to work with investors buying UK properties to guide them through the entire process, from help with buying properties at discounted values via auctions, managing the refurbishment, appointing advisers and even managing the property and collecting rent if required.

TAX CONSIDERATIONS IF BUYING FROM OVERSEAS

There are taxes that must be considered during when buying property from overseas. For example:

a. Nonresident landlords (you live 6 months or more abroad) must pay income tax on the rental income they received.
b. When buying, there is a tax called Stamp Duty which is an important cost that must be considered. If the property is a second buy-to-let investment, as of the

writing of this book the Stamp Duty was structured as below.

Up to £125,000 – 3% rate. £125,001 to £250,000 – 5% rate. £250,001 – £925,000 – 8% rate. £925,001 to £1,500,000 – 13% rate. Above £1,500,000 – 15% rate. For example, if your property is worth £200,000, you will have to pay 3% on 125,000 and 5% on the other 75,000. That is £7,500 stamp duty.

c. Council tax: depending on the 'band' every property is classified at, a sum would have to be paid which can vary from £100 a month to £1000. This tax basically goes to pay the expenses of the local government, police, rubbish collection, etc.

SELLING YOUR PROPERTY FROM ABROAD

If you need to sell your property, you must take into account the following:

a. You will have to pay Capital Gains Taxes if you are selling your property. Such gains are the increase of the value of the property taking away buying, purchasing, improvement and any disposal costs.
b. Such money must be paid within 30 days of completion of the sale.

c. The current tax level, as of the writing of this book is 28%.

In summary, you can buy property from abroad being a non-British nonresident landlord, but make sure you your follow a strict due diligence which allows you to forecast your potential income and if possible, the capital gains you can realize from each project. Remember this:

A professional investor starts with the exit strategy in mind.

4 STRATEGIES YOU CAN USE TO BOOST YOUR PROFITS FROM PROPERTY

By Jorge Lombana

The First strategy, which is working really, really well is called **'Service Accommodation'**, this is where you rent your property on a short-term basis and through different channels such as **booking.com, Airbnb, Trivago,** you name it.

You've got hundreds of different websites that you can rent your property through. The type of renters you will get are for example holiday makers, or people who are coming on business, they only need your property for a few days, perhaps a couple of weeks, and obviously they will pay a premium, because they know this is only for a few days, so these strategies work more like a hotel kind of thing basis, so that is one of the most profitable ones in the business at the moment.

Apart from the financial rewards of the **Service Accommodation** strategy, you also have some additional benefits such as:

- You know that the property won't be rented the full month and therefore the wear and tear will take longer to show.
- Your property is being cleaned every time a person checks out ensure its upkeep.
- This pattern allows you to constantly inspect your asset which gives you more control.
- You don't have to deal with evictions.
- You don't have to chase rent as these because everything is done and paid up front.

On top of that, everything is automatically done through the websites that provide the service. It's just an excellent strategy. All you need to do is just make sure you market the property at its full potential, so you've got the maximum occupancy each month. If done correctly, you can potentially double sometimes more, the rental income that you would get using other strategies.

So that's one of my favorite strategies at the moment.

The second strategy that I use quite a lot is called '**Rent-to-Rent**' and it's basically giving your property to an operator who will pay you a guaranteed rent taking care of the bills and everything else. Some companies even offer to pay for minor repairs, getting it very close to an ideal hands-off investment generating real passive income.

I love it because I know that once I give one of my properties to one of these companies I know that they will handle absolutely everything and I will have to just sit back and relax and get my income from them. It's not difficult at all and it's a huge, huge strategy to maximize your profit.

The third strategy I use quite often is called '**Flips**'. A flip is basically buying a property and refurbishing it to a higher standard. This strategy is especially powerful at generating big chunks of money in a short period of time which could potentially help you to fill your investment pot and expand your portfolio or support other projects that need cash.

And the fourth and last strategy, which is in fact my favorite one, is the House in Multiple Occupation or HMO for short. HMO is just amazing just for the size of income that the property can bring compared to a normal strategy. However it does have its own downsides such as it requires a lot more time to manage and attention. Also, an effort will have to be put into trying to fill every single room which includes avoiding any void periods but ultimately it's one of the biggest and highest in terms of return.

Also, once you have an HMO and it's fully licensed, the property itself can be valued as a business rather than brick and mortar. What that means in practical terms is that the equity value increases which you could 'release' by remortgaging the HMO. If done correctly, it can lead to a big cash injection you can now use to expand your portfolio.

It's a very good strategy but you need to know how to do it and where to do it because it doesn't always work in all areas. That is why your research is so important: you must ensure you're targeting the right people in the right areas for this particular strategy.

GETTING AN HMO LICENSE

It could be stressful, but if you meet all the requirements that an HMO license needs, you're pretty much covered.

The requirements will vary from council to council but they are mostly related to Health and Safety, building, control, building regulations, and fire safety (that is one of the biggest requirements) from councils: to make sure that you have all your fire alarms in place, that you've got your fire doors, your fire frames, the property is fully wired with the fire alarm, and all the alarms are interconnected just to make sure that you also have your fire escapes and your windows meeting the standards. Also, the comfort of the people living there is important for local authorities, for example, the rooms in the building have a minimum size. All these are critical to meet HMO standards and get a license. It's completely different to build an HMO than to just refurbish a normal house, so it's very important to have a clear plan right from the beginning as such a plan will be reflected at a deep level in the way you redesign and improve your property.

Understanding what the needs are to get an HMO license from the beginning of your refurbishment and make sure you've included them in the building layout. Your developer and your builders must understand what is required and the purpose of the property. As in every business communication is essential to avoid costly mistakes.

.

HOW I USED A COMBINATION OF THESE STRATEGIES TO BECOME FINANCIALLY FREE IN 4 YEARS

By Jorge Lombana

When I look back and analyze what I have done so far to achieve my financial freedom through UK property, I can see a very interesting path that you too can follow. I call this the Lombana Ladder. It has taken me over a decade to put it together and it is a vision I have not fulfilled completely yet.

See below and illustration of the Lombana Ladder.

```
          /\
         /  \
        /Developer\
       /   Flips   \
      /    HMOs     \
     /    Service    \
    /  Accomodation   \
   /   Rent to Rent    \
  /_____\
```

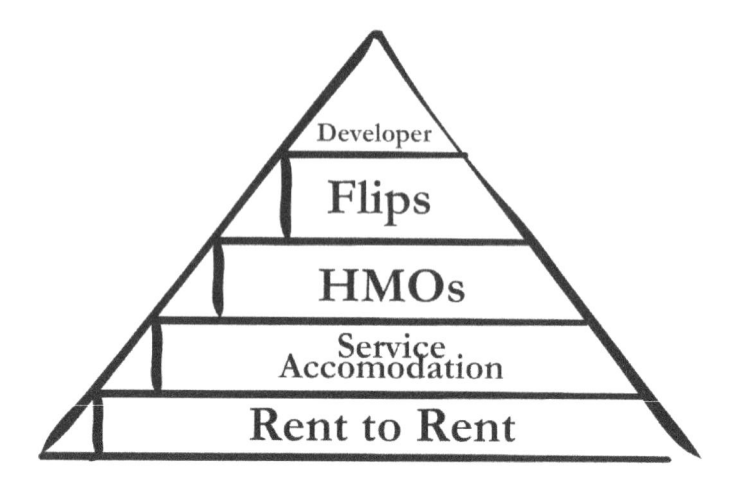

Figure 3. Lombana Ladder

In case you're wondering, this is a pyramid and not a ladder; this is why: I call it as such because the way it works: each rung is required to be able to move upwards to the next one.

I started renting rooms from properties which didn't even belong to me. All legally done, by the way, with the consent of the owner. Nowadays I have many houses producing recurrent income for me giving me very good financial muscle.

The second strategy I then used was Service Accommodation. You can see is a variation of Rent to Rent but, given the right conditions, more money can be made here than through the normal model.

The financial leverage of these two strategies working together with cash I raised from other investors (i.e. Family and friends) were fundamental to get to the third rung of the ladder: buying property of my own and becoming the direct landlord doing my own HMOs. By doing so, I got access to two important things: higher recurrent revenue and access to capital via my Lombana Property Speed Cycle (LPSC) as explained before. This is the fourth rung of the ladder, Flips and conversions (i.e., converting commercial units into residential units, taking a large property and converting it into separate flats with separate leases).

This is the stage where I am at the moment. The next step I envision I will take is to become a developer and to build from scratch, acquiring land and doing my own developments. It will not be long before I am able to do it. From experience I know for a fact that there is even more money to be made right there.

Something I want you to notice is that my goal is to invest for cash flow using the LPSC to boost my portfolio by leveraging capital gains from property improvement. This is how I got my financial freedom just before my 30s. You can also do it; your age doesn't matter.

If you want to accelerate your journey, go now to www.propertystrategist.co.uk/ to learn more or get in contact with us at **info@propertystrategist.co.uk**. Also you can send us a text on **07411904124** (00447411904124 outside the UK) and we will call you back.

CREATIVE WAYS OF RAISING CAPITAL

By Jorge Lombana

One of the main questions people very often ask me when it comes to Property is this one: How can I get the money to get started? My answer normally is another question (kind of an educational one), I tell them they need to start asking themselves a different one:

How can I get creative and actually come up with the money that I need for investment?

That is one of the biggest things as a property investor: The way you come up with financing.

Finance is one of the pillars in this business and not only because finance will give you the leverage that you need to come up with the money to buy properties, but also, it will leverage the amount of money that you have to potentially rapidly expand your portfolio.

So, one of the easiest ways to come up with funds is just *friends and family*, people that are willing to lend you X or

Y or Z amount of money and then you can potentially put that towards an investment. People that you know, your family or friends or your social circle that have liquidity sitting in a bank account getting only 1 or 2 or 3 percent interest. You could potentially offer them higher return to get them onboard.

Another ways is to use your *credit cards*, make sure you have a good available balance on your credit card that you know that you could potentially use towards a property, your overdrafts and anything that you know that potentially could help you to build up that capital to start climbing the property ladder.

SPOTTING THE RIGHT LOCATION IN THE UK

By Jorge Lombana

First of all you need to identify the city. You would be amazed what you can learn by reading news and also what you can learn from local and financial reports on how;

- A particular city is doing financially.
- How the population is growing.
- How the type of investments and how much money is the city actually producing.

You can find all these reports in the Financial Times, you can find more of these reports in home magazines and investors' magazines. They will show particular places where the highest deals are achieved in the UK.

Once you find your ideal city where you want to invest, what I personally do in an area or in a city that I'm kind of new to, I just go to the local Estate Agent, bring a map and

I sit down with one of them as if I was going to buy a property today. I ask, 'Where would you recommend buying? Estate Agents know streets inside out, so they know exactly what's going on in the local areas. They're the best and more qualified people to tell you, where and what spots to find.

A second question I will ask them is this one: 'If you were to invest your own money and to buy a house tomorrow, where would you invest it and why?'... They will tell me exactly what particular roads, area or close to what particular shop, stadium, hospital, school and even of a new development will take place there. Also, they may know about big companies employing large amounts of people. In other words, they will give you a key piece of information which is the size of demand for properties in certain area.

Once you've got that information, then you just look for the property in a laser-focused manner with a high certainty that your property will be rented quickly once you finish the development.

One of the best aspects here is that all that information is absolutely free, all you need to do is just build a good rapport with Property agents, go in very friendly and ask, 'Look, I'm a new investor in this area and I would like to buy a 2 or 3 bedroom property' and then as I said, just bring a map with you and get them to circle where they would buy Property.

From there you say, 'Do you have anything available at the moment?' and they will show you a few properties that they might have in the area and that's where your property journey starts.

WHAT CAN GO WRONG?

By Jorge Lombana

There are a number of things that can go wrong if you don't follow the approach I have suggested above. Remember I have learnt from experience, making mistakes… but it doesn't have to be that way for you.

Your Research, Power Team and Financing must be in place. Without them there can be some costly problems, such as, for example, having to stop your development because you run out of cash (but you have done everything else right).

Sometimes people think that they can do everything on their own; however you always need people next to you to help you out, to guide you and to put you on the right track through the right investment and potential things that can go wrong, for example:

- Not buying the right property,
- Not knowing that the property has got some serious structural issues.
- The property maybe 'Listed' which means structural modifications are heavily restricted.

- Lease issues as to who owns the land and what you can do with the property.

All these can be tremendously expensive to fix.

For example, a new property with structural issues will require a fully qualified team of builders with knowledge of building regulations, a structural engineer and maybe even need permission from the council to change it. In the UK, the older the property, the higher the likelihood of it of being protected (Listed) by the local authorities.

So things like that will cause quite a lot of money to escape your hands decreasing your projected ROI. You must avoid them at all costs and to do so, you need the right knowledge to spot them. For example, when you're doing viewings and that's probably one of the biggest mistakes people can make in the process.

Another way things can go wrong, which is quite common, is builders. I can't stress enough how important it is to have the right team. Builders can take a lot longer than they told you they would; the project can cost a lot more money than initially planned. There are things along the way that may go wrong which will eat away at your budget and by the time you've realized it you may have run out of funds. Not a situation you want to be in. You need to make sure the property is a state where it can be refurbished, with that on hand and the right builders to help you out in that process; you will have one of the most important pieces of the puzzle.

Finally, your Estate Agents. They are the ones who are going to provide the income for you, the ones that are going to be working very, very hard to try to get those properties rented and those rooms filled to make the expected return for you. Therefore, you need to pay them well; you need to know who the right agent is to manage your property. For instance, all agents will tell you, 'Yes, we'll do this, we'll do that', but when you start working with them, the management isn't what you expected, the property is not well looked after, there are rooms available or the property can experience some void periods. That is a big thing and it will hurt your return on investment.

You need to make sure you find the right person to rent your properties, make sure your legal team is a professional one to spot any potential problems that the property may have. A good team of builders may spot any major issues early in the process and avoid costs.

My best piece of advice is to surround yourself with people to guide you on where to invest and how to invest and what potential problems to avoid.

MORE ABOUT YOUR POWER TEAM

By Jorge Lombana

A good power team its absolutely essential in this business, so first of all is your **solicitor**, your solicitors are the ones that are going to cover you in any type of problems that may arise during the purchase of the property, they will also protect you against any people, any person trying to sue you over anything related to the investment, so they're really, really important. Just make sure they act fast because speed in property is one of the most important things you can have so having a good legal team is essential.

Second, Builders, but just not any builders, the right type of builders: people who are reliable, fast enough (speed

'Speed in property is one of the most important aspects you can have'

again), a team who will work closely with you and can come back if any repairs need to be done. Even if it's after the refurbishment. As with any team, you must be able to trust them: you know they are trying to finish the project as soon as possible because they know the longer it takes the lower will be the ROI.

You also need your **Estate Agents**. They're essential. Those are the ones that, as I said earlier), are going to bring you the revenue on the property so make sure they've got a track record of properties that they're rented or sold, not just a one-thing man, they kind of like tend to think that they know how to manage property and eventually they just don't, so a reliable Estate Agent is important, they will look after the property, report any maintenance issues, collect your rents and most importantly, they will fill the property or the rooms at all times so that is very important.

Finally you need to have your **Lender**. Make sure you have your broker (that is what your lender normally does) who can provide the financing that you need to buy the properties. The financing that you need to buy quickly. Sometimes mortgages are not quick enough: you need to close your deals between 28 days to a maximum 6 weeks.

A good broker may be able find you alternative ways to raise financing including *bridge loans*, *short term loans* or some *private loans* that can potentially be lent against any other property or assets you may already have, accelerating the process so the money is found in 2 or 3 weeks. Currently in the UK that's a very quick turnaround to find financing.

Those are the most important teams that you need to have, and once you have those 4 angles covered, you're pretty much set to go.

It takes time to build a good relationship with Brokers, making sure they give you the right rates and the right finance. Also your Builder is very important, make sure you trust them, make sure they're reliable, make sure that you've got a good relationship with them, your Estate Agent once again and your legal team.

RIGHT RATES FOR A LOAN

Some mortgages will vary in terms of the loaned value as a percentage of the equity of the property as well as the rates you will get.

Currently, most mortgages will give you between 75 to 80% equity loaned value and rates will vary from lender to lender, but you can expect anything between 1% and to 6-7 % per annum. The rates you get depend strongly on your credit score: The better the credit score you have, the better rates the bank will give you. It really depends on your personal circumstances.

WHAT IF YOUR CREDIT SCORE IS NOT GOOD?

If you don't have a good track record in your credit score then there are other alternatives that you can use and other lenders (not necessarily at the top of my list of financing sources) such as private lenders or off-street lenders that could potentially raise money for you on a slightly higher interest rate. In this case you would be looking at the top of the range mentioned before, that is from 5% to 7%. So it can be done if your credit score is not the best, however your return on investment will be lower. That is why you must take care of that track record.

Everything you do with money in the UK (and really, anywhere in the world) is tracked and whether you know it or not, your financial behavior is measured at every step by financial institutions, lenders and brokers.

TYPES OF FINANCING AVAILABLE

There are a few types of ways to raise financing. First of all, we'll just stand mortgage, we'll just buy the property, put 25% down and the bank will offer you 75% of the value of the property, so that's probably one of the most common and the most used ones.

One that I use quite a lot is *bridging finance*. This type of strategy is a short term finance loan where you need to pay money back quickly, anywhere from 1 month to 2 years. The downside here is that the interest rate you will get is a lot higher than a normal mortgage. This type of loan is done against an asset (secure loan): They will lend you against the property that you're currently buying. So for example, if you're buying a property that is worth £100,000 they will lend you 75% of it and you will have to come up with the rest.

In this case that is £25,000. On some occasions, they will require a valuation, in some cases they don't, and the finance could be raised literally within a couple of weeks to 3 weeks, so it's a straightforward process, fairly quickly.

Using this strategy you can close a Property deal within a few weeks. Again the speedy investor eats the slow one.

You can also get financing from your **credit card**, if you've got a good limit on your credit card, you could potentially pay a property deposit on a credit card. You can also use it to transfer cash from your credit card into your bank account, which is called a **cash transfer** in the credit card world's language. Bear in mind that, not all credit cards approve this, but if you have a good one which allows you to do it, it's a very good way to raise cash.

Another way to raise money is through (as I said before) friends, family and people that may have some 'Unused cash' they're not really doing anything with it. To convince them to come onboard you could say argue things such as 'I am currently starting a new project in Property, I could give you a 6, 7% return on that investment compared to the 2 or 3% that you're getting from the bank'. This is one of the strategies I used to start my property career.

Another creative way is to use your overdraft. Speak to your banks, and try to increase it. This strategy, together with increasing the limit of your credit card can be combined to get more access to capital. Obviously, you need to be careful and put all your present and future income and expenses together so you ensure you can manage the situation.

I've always said that in business you need to use the maximum amount of credit that you can to finance your properties. That is called leverage. Operating this way has worked really well for me and I'm pretty sure it will work really well with other people if they know how to use the credit responsibly.

YOU WANT TO INVEST, AND GET RESULTS FAST BUT DON'T HAVE ANY EXPERIENCE

By Jorge Lombana

Some people like to learn the hard way and take a long time to 'prepare'. I can tell you, there are plenty of courses around of people offering anything from mentorships to just particular courses in particular topics, courses in just different things in particular or legals, so there's a lot of information out there. There are also a lot of videos on YouTube that you can listen to and see it may work for you. However…

Currently mentorship courses are charging anything between £15-20,000 to get you started on the property ladder. That is way too much to pay to someone for the amount of work that they're going to do. You need to find a reliable person that can take you on the property journey that can take by the hand and show you step-by-step what to do. Once you walk that path once, all you need to do is just to rinse and repeat, over and over again. This is how you will get you to grow your portfolio and achieve financial freedom. That is, whatever you call financial freedom: may it be 2 houses, 3, 4, 5 or 10 houses. Whatever the number in your head is, once you know the strategy, you will need to simply 'copy and paste' until you get there.

We, me and my Power Team, work with all sorts of investors. We take people by the hand do absolutely everything for them: we take care of the sourcing the property, make sure it's in the right location, that it's the type of property that will bring the return you are after.

We provide you with all the legals through my own personal solicitors who have handled hundreds of deals in the UK by now.

We have a team of reliable builders doing full management of the building works and refurbishments. We basically make sure everything is up to standards; it is carried out to the best possible way and quite fast.

Finally we ensure you get the return expected at the end of the process by renting out your property to the right people. This is done through our proven and tested team of Estate Agents.

We do all these things for our investors, helping them to either start investing in the UK property ladder or to expand their portfolio faster by strategically investing in high potential locations, navigating the tremendous difference in prices across this country. We do this with investors who live in the UK and investors who live abroad. Both British Citizens and non-citizens.

WHAT IF I DON'T WANT TO MANAGE THE PROPERTY?

We also do the management; we've got a few agencies that currently take over this side of the business for our own properties. We would normally work closely with them so the property is professionally kept so you don't have go through the headaches of dealing with tenants, repairs or payment collections. The whole system is arranged so even after the agency's fees, the investor still receives the return agreed.

FOUR SUCCESSFUL INVESTMENT EXAMPLES

By Jorge Lombana

Investment 1:

6 Canon Road
Purchase price £55k
Renovations £33k
Rent £19200
ROI = 21%

This was a large 3 bedroom terrace house property which we converted into a 6 bedroom and 3 Bathroom HMO.

The loft already existed with no more use than as storage space.

We created some partition walls so we could make 2 bedrooms and 1 bathroom in the loft. Then we relocated the existing bathroom and rearranged it to make the extra bedrooms.

We also made a double set of kitchens to provide enough for the tenants.

The property is now rented on a rent to rent deal which brings revenue of £19.200 per annum.

Investment 2:

37 Valley Road
Purchase price £70k
3 bedrooms and 1 bathroom
Converted into 5 bedrooms and 2 bathrooms HMO
Renovations £16k
ROI= 21.6%

It was converted from a 3 bedroom house to a 5 bedroom and 2 bathroom HMO.

It is now rented on a room by room basis bringing in revenue of £18600 per annum.

This property has received a valuation of £135k

Investment 3:

12 Dinorwick road
Purchase price £34k
Renovations £23k
3 bedrooms and 1 bathroom converted into 4 bedrooms and 2 bathrooms.
ROI = 27%

This property only had 2 good size bedrooms, despite being a large property.

We moved the existing bathroom to create more space on the small room.

The kitchen was extended and made open plan, creating an open space and a modern taste.

This property is rented on a room by room basis and it's bringing in revenue of £15600 per annum.

Four Successful Investment Examples

Investment 4:

30 Robarts Road Purchase price £56k
3 bedroom property/1 bathroom
Converted into 6 bedroom HMO with 2 bathrooms.
Renovations £32k
ROI = 17%

It was converted into a 6 bedroom. A few walls were rearranged to make extra bedrooms and bathrooms.

Figure 4. Kitchen at Cannon Road Property before and after

The basement was converted into a living room therefore utilising every single inch of the property.

The property is now worth £150k and bringing in a steady income of £1250 per month on a rent to rent deal.

SO, HOW TO INVEST IN THE UK AT THE BEST PRICES AND BEST FINANCING RATES AVAILABLE?

(Have we answered the question?)

By Noel Cardona

Before we finish and tell you more about what investors we have worked with are saying and our own stories (see next two chapters). I would like to make sure you have answered the initial question we promised on the cover of this book.

Investing in UK Property in at the best prices means probably taking advantage of high growth areas outside the area of London. Can you invest in the Capital? Absolutely! But you will need stronger financial muscle.

The strategies we use can be applied to any UK city.

To invest at the best rates you must take care of your own credit score as well as start building good relationships with lenders, as you go about proving your capacity as an investor you will have quicker access to cash (the speed concept) and better rates. If you have your own money and don't have to go to a lender then you pay no fees!

However, prices and rates are just half of the picture as you need to understand your exit strategy: Capital gains or Cash Flow and ensure that you have a realistic target ROI for your property.

A high ROI can accommodate high interest rates and prices if necessary.

Last but not least, do not forget the human side. Investing in Property to create wealth in a professional way will require a mindset that can cope with high amounts of debt in leverage, good finance management as it gets more and more complex and a clear objective of what your overall strategy is.

We wish you the best of luck with you investments and if you ever want to contact us, you can do so at info@propertystrategist.co.uk or send us a text to the mobile number 07411904124 (0047411904124 outside the UK).

WHAT INVESTORS ARE SAYING…

Jorge and I went to University together and spend a few years studying. A few years later I was working for the NHS while Jorge had changed careers and he was working in property. We then had a chat and I mentioned that I wanted to join him and he accepted. We then created a company with another partner that has now been operating for 3 years and we expect the revenue for the next financial year to exceed £700k.

We have bought a few properties in Liverpool which most of them bring a steady income and a huge return of over 15% on most cases.

We are very excited about the bright future and I am looking forward to what's coming next!

Aeron Logan
Investor and entrepreneur
London.

What Investors Are Saying

'I have known Jorge over the last 7 years. I approached him to get to know what he was doing and was fascinated with how property can provide a passive income and how I could become financially free. I have had a music shop for a few years and it requires a lot of my own time. I wanted something that allowed me to spend more time with my kids and Jorge showed me how to do it.

I bought 2 flats in Liverpool. Jorge always says that we had to add value to the property no matter what. So we made one extra bedroom and redecorated the whole bathroom to give it a luxurious feel to it and installed a brand new kitchen.

Both flats are now rented through a company that operates them as service accommodation and I'm getting a guaranteed rent for 3 years of £850 per flat.

It couldn't get any better than that!

I am looking to get some more funds to do it all again'

Deicola Ferrer Neto
London

JORGE LOMBANA – WHO AM I ANYWAY?

I am a professional Property investor and entrepreneur. I initially started my career back in 2009, renting out rooms as a way to create extra sources of income. I then moved on to other small businesses that started along the way, including selling dry fruit, nuts, sweets in one of London's underground *stations*.

Next I moved on to open a new business specializing in printing all sorts of merchandise including T-shirts, mugs, fashionable clothing and any other sorts of merchandise and equipment for companies.

At the same time, I started thinking about Property and how it was probably the best investment I could possibly make. At the same time I was still working full-time and generating extra income by renting rooms.

Eventually I realized that I was not going to be financially free if I kept being an employee. So... I thought to myself, well, if I would start doing and working the amount of hours that I do as an employee, I could potentially do the same for my own business.

It was then when I initially started to focus more on Property and tried to push property to the next level the way I've always dreamt.

MY TRACK RECORD AS AN INVESTOR

I started back in 2009 renting rooms just to get a side income to complement my day job. I've always known that having a side income is always good, not only for the facility of being able to save more but also knowing if that side income grows more than your salary; that's the point where you can kind of start moving away from your job.

So that was one of the first investments that I started to make. I first bought a flat in the neighborhood where I lived and I thought that… that was a very good investment back then. However I quickly realized it was not because I was paying for that property from my income, so I decided to go to courses to try to educate myself financially and then that's when I started realizing the actual investment is when the property pays for itself and leaves you a side income. That is when I realized that I needed to start buying properties pretty much straight away.

I was researching the market realizing the properties were extremely, extremely high, there wasn't enough profit to be made and the amount of investment needed to go through that property was quite substantial, so I started looking for different alternatives, including other countries, including perhaps other cities within the UK, but wasn't sure at the time where to invest or how to start.

I started investigating a little bit more, doing a little bit more research in the whole UK, trying to find the best spots to invest and eventually I found out the North of England was probably one of the best places to invest right now, not only for the lack of growth that the North of England was experiencing a few years ago, but also the amount of investment that was going through it at the moment, not only by private investments but also by the government and some private equities firms which were pouring a lot of money into that area, not taking into account the amount of infrastructure that it's getting from the government to try to connect the South of England to other areas, in particularly London, all the way to the North of England with the High Speed 2, the High Speed 3 is a massive project that hopefully will be completed in the next 6-7 years.

This endeavor has brought an extraordinary amount of money into the economy of the Northwest of England. Not only that, but also the amount of investment going through the docks, in particular in Liverpool, one of my favorite cities to invest in, taking into account that the old docks are being refurbished and upgraded to try to get those ports back into their days of glory, where all the big ships used to come to Liverpool and all the cruise ships, bringing a lot of tourism, new jobs, employment, a lot of immigration and just more than you can make it as a whole.

Eventually I found the perfect spot to invest in and I bought the first property, then after a few months a second, third and fourth one, eventually generating enough income to really get me started growing my investments and increasing the speed which I was investing. Today, I currently have 16 properties, 13 of which are currently rented and all providing all full income, the last 3 is a development that I'm currently converting from a massive house, into a 6 one-bedroom house, well 6 one-bedroom flat and that is a joint venture that I did with one of my partners, he's taken 3 properties of that investment and I've taken the other 3, so that, as of the writing of this book, is under refurbishment and will be completed in the next 3-4 months, potentially, that will be my sixteenth property completed.

From there, I'm looking to exponentially grow my portfolio, not just by buying properties, but to actually start developing which is one of the nicest, probably juiciest parts of the business where you can get substantially more income and money out of these investments.

At the moment, I'm currently working with investors as well trying to help them achieve that financial freedom that they have always looked for. I am also helping them invest other savings or any potential money that they would like to put towards a good deal. I would suggest 3 or 4 different types of investments and then from there, what we do is to try to do the hard work on their behalf and manage the whole process of

- sourcing the properties,
- Purchasing,
- Doing all the legal for the property.

Once the property is purchased we then go into the refurbishment which we will manage 100% and then rent it out in the open market and at the end just provide that return of investment that was agreed to with the investor when we first started.

In the last couple of years, we have already managed the purchase of 189 properties in the UK with investors from both the UK and non UK based individuals.

CAN YOU USE MY STRATEGIES TO INVEST?

The majority of investors I work with are just people in their mid 30's to 50-60's who potentially have been employed for most of their lives.

They have some savings set side and don't really know where to invest it or how to invest it and they want something secure, but who are also looking for a high rate on investment.

I have tried different businesses myself: I have invested my own money into the stock market and other side businesses but I always came back to property and that's what I tell all my investors.

Property not only gives you that financial security that you know that if anything goes wrong you'll still have the property there, that you can always sell and try to recover most of your money compared to putting your money into any sort of investment that if any crisis happen, you could potentially lose it all. In contrast, you always have your property there, and if you sell it at the right time, you can always make a profit out of it, if not, you can always hold it and get rental income.

Now, every investor is different, every investor has a different type of risk and different expectations, length of time they would like to invest for and obviously a different budget of how much they would like to invest towards a particular property, and also, every investor has a particular return of investment that they expect at the end of the project.

So, we work in a variety of ways, and we always try to fulfill the investors' expectations, especially the return that he will get at the end to the budget that is going to be used towards these particular investments.

I would say there's nothing in the investors; what we have is people who are interested in putting the income of that savings towards a project, and we help them achieve just that.

So like this is not something you need to have a massive amount of money for, all you need to have is enough money to cover the process of the property, and the refurbishment, the rest will be finance, but we can always help you out to achieve the financing for the property, and show you the way how from that initial finance, you can then release equity from the property, in a couple of years' time, so we'll take you through a journey not just when we start but also along the way until you require us to do so.

NOEL CARDONA – WHO AM I ANYWAY?

www.propertystrategist.co.uk

'Business Coach for the Elite'. Hi, I am Noel Cardona, when you work with me I give you access to tested and proven strategies learned from my 10+ years as an entrepreneur, investor, author and speaker to accelerate your journey towards freedom, wealth and prosperity. I have been mentored myself by some of the best entrepreneurs in the world having access to cutting edge tools and lessons which the average failing entrepreneur will never get access to. People I don't normally work with are the negative thinkers, who are looking for approval and not advice, if you think that your business is different, then my advice won't work for you.

I am the most practical business mentor, coach, teacher you will ever meet. I am a plain speaking, direct and upfront bloke who walks his talk and delivers on what he promises – EVERY time. If you are ready to take serious advice contact me at info@propertystrategist.co.uk.

OTHER BOOKS BY NOEL

I have published seven books on entrepreneurship, personal growth and business excellence. If you want to see them all please go to *propertystrategist.co.uk.* While you are there join my list so we can start communicating continuously.

The Mental Breakfast

The Mental Breakfast is a tremendous system for you to take charge over your own will and make your productivity go through the ceiling. There is so much more to increasing your capacity to deliver than just playing the 'being busy' game. This book shows you the basis and also the method to be able to achieve two things. One, not to forget your dreams so you keep aligned and two, your alignment is maintained in the long term and not just for the first week of the year as happens to 99% of the population. This book talks about a breakthrough concept: Before you achieve Financial Freedom you must achieve Mental Freedom. I know for a fact that only a few people who read this book will have the courage to implement it! Will you be one of them?

Intentional Winner

Intentional Winner shows you what the zero baseline for success is. It helps you understand how you need to think and act in order to start your journey to whatever you define as success. Also, it is a must read for those who have been on this path for a while but don't seem to make any progress. Becoming an Intentional Winner requires knowledge of yourself and knowledge of a proven successful method that leads you faster towards your goals. Being successful is not necessarily becoming a millionaire; there are a lot more things to success than that. Intentional Winner talks about 5 drivers you need to learn and use to steer your life in the right direction.

Lightning Source UK Ltd.
Milton Keynes UK
UKHW021148290322
400778UK00008B/1703